Sunrise

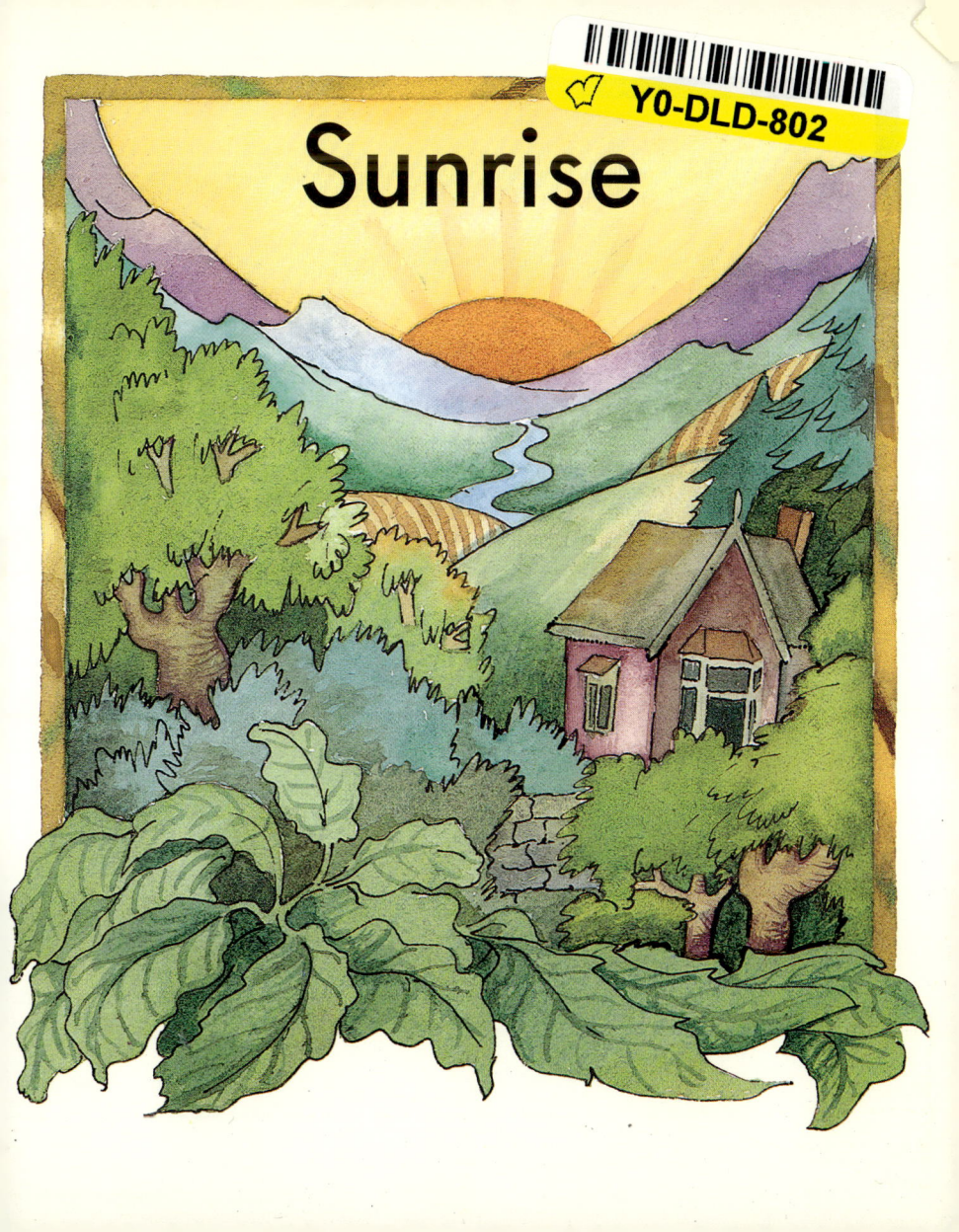

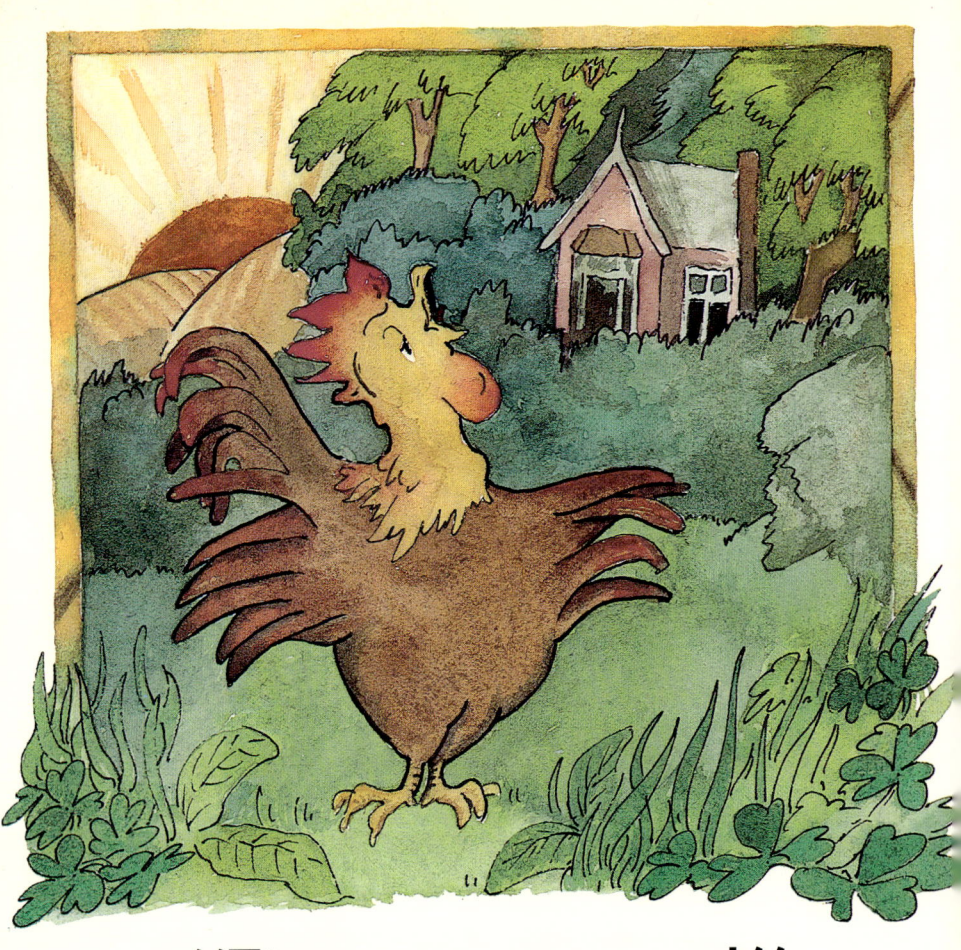

"Time to get up!"
said the rooster.

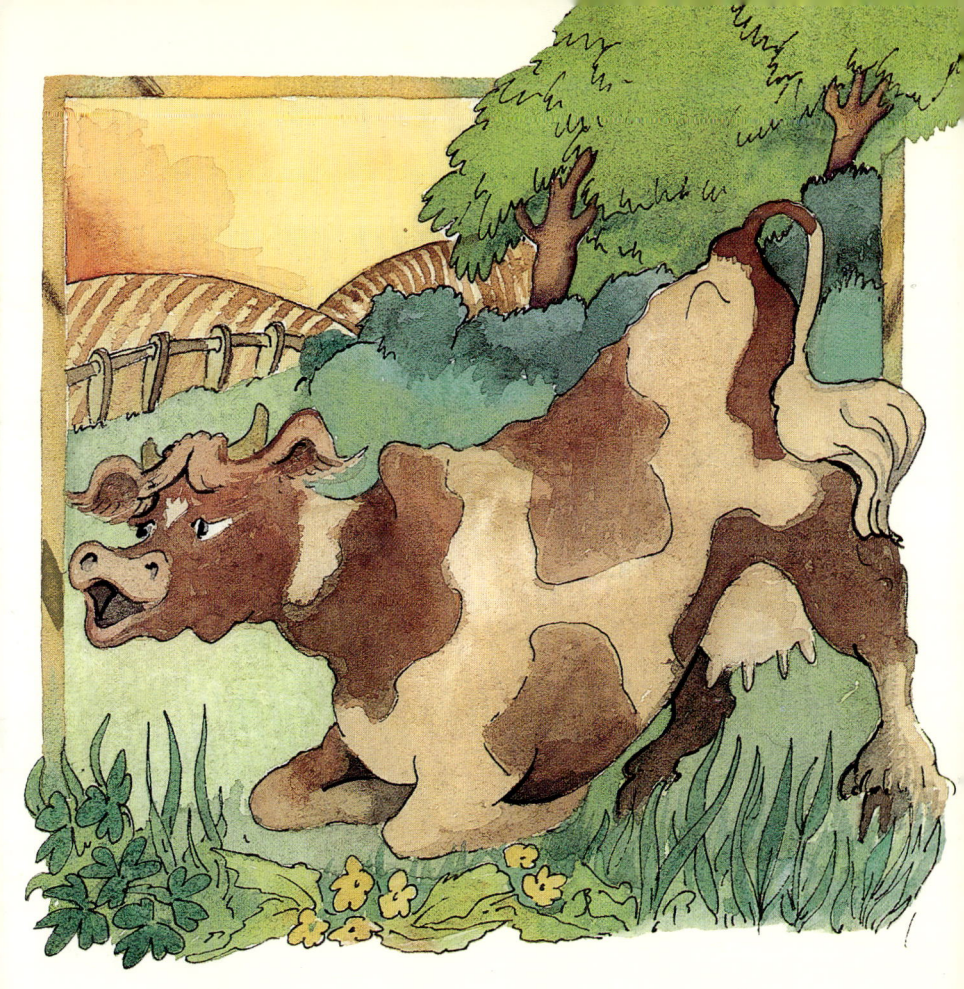

"Time to get up!"
said the cow.

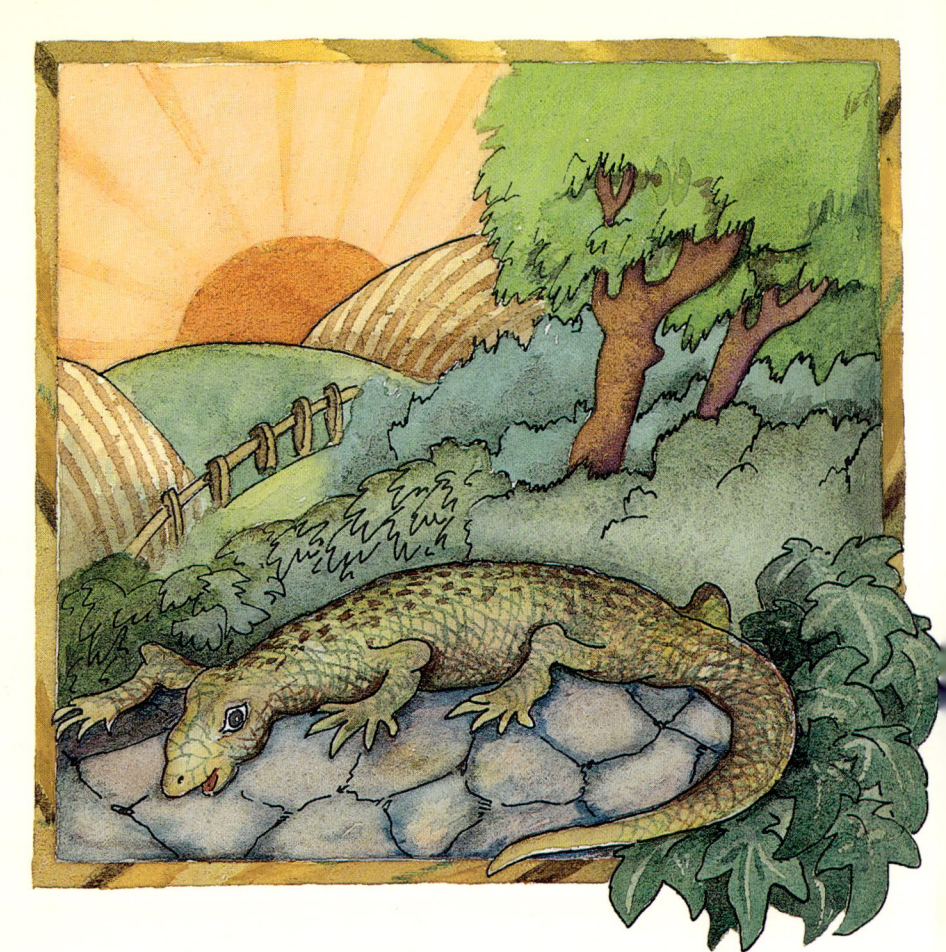

"Time to get up!"
said the lizard.

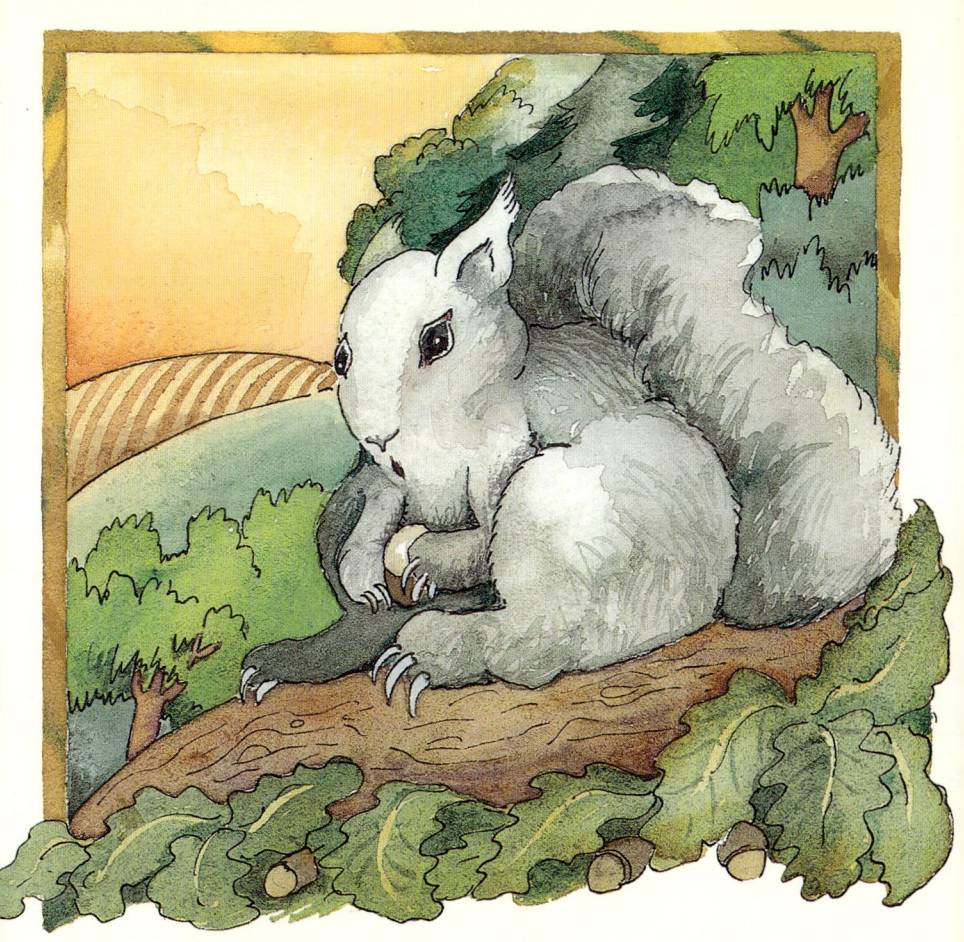

"Time to get up!"
said the squirrel.

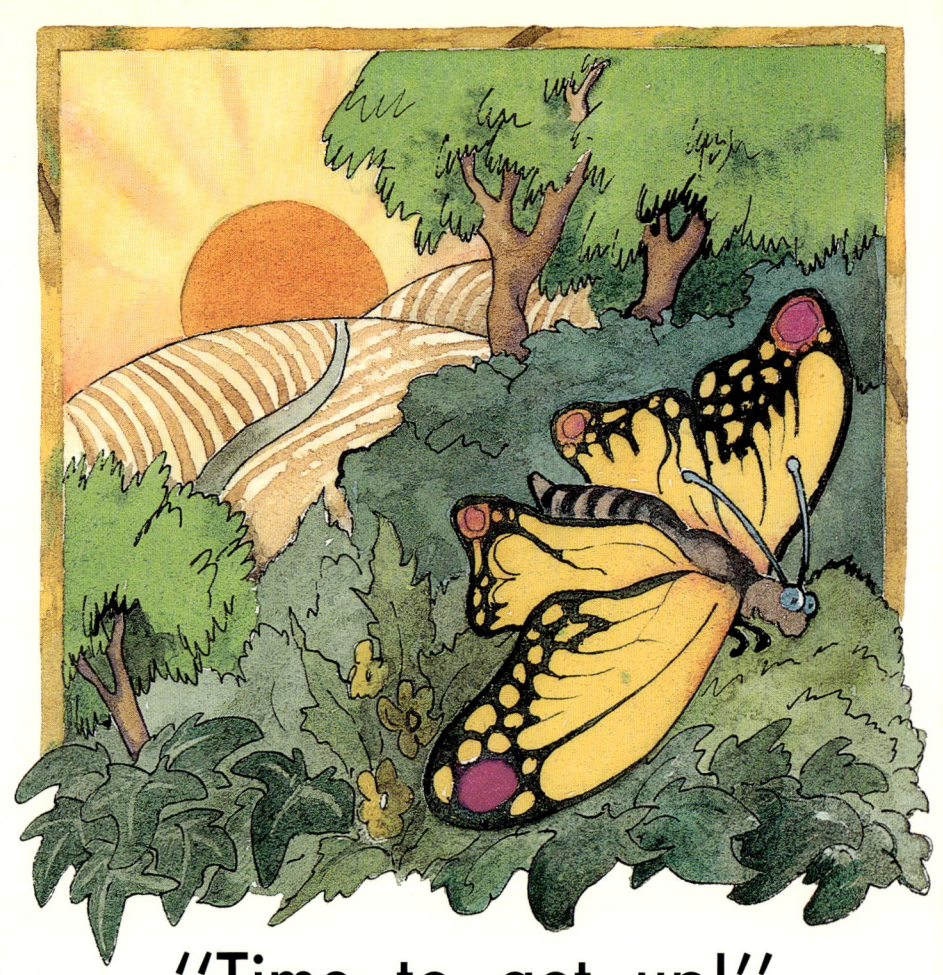

"Time to get up!"
said the butterfly.

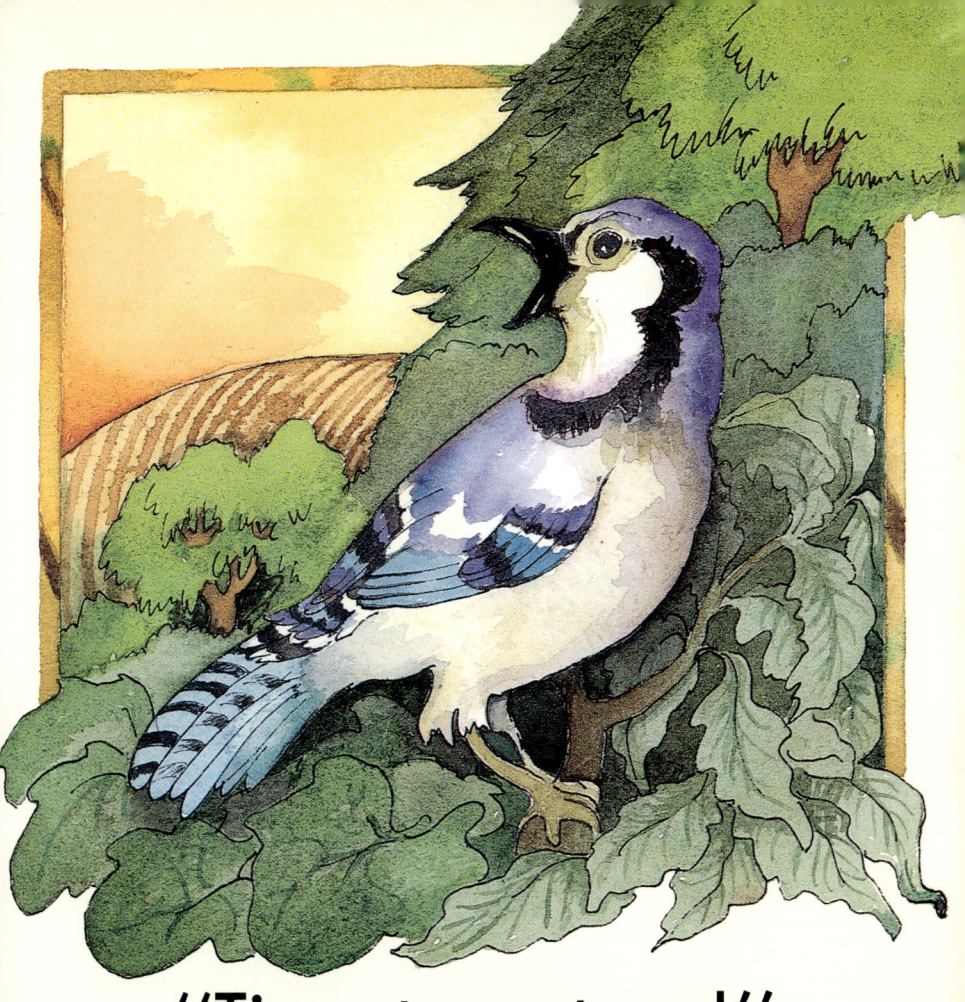

"Time to get up!"
said the bird.

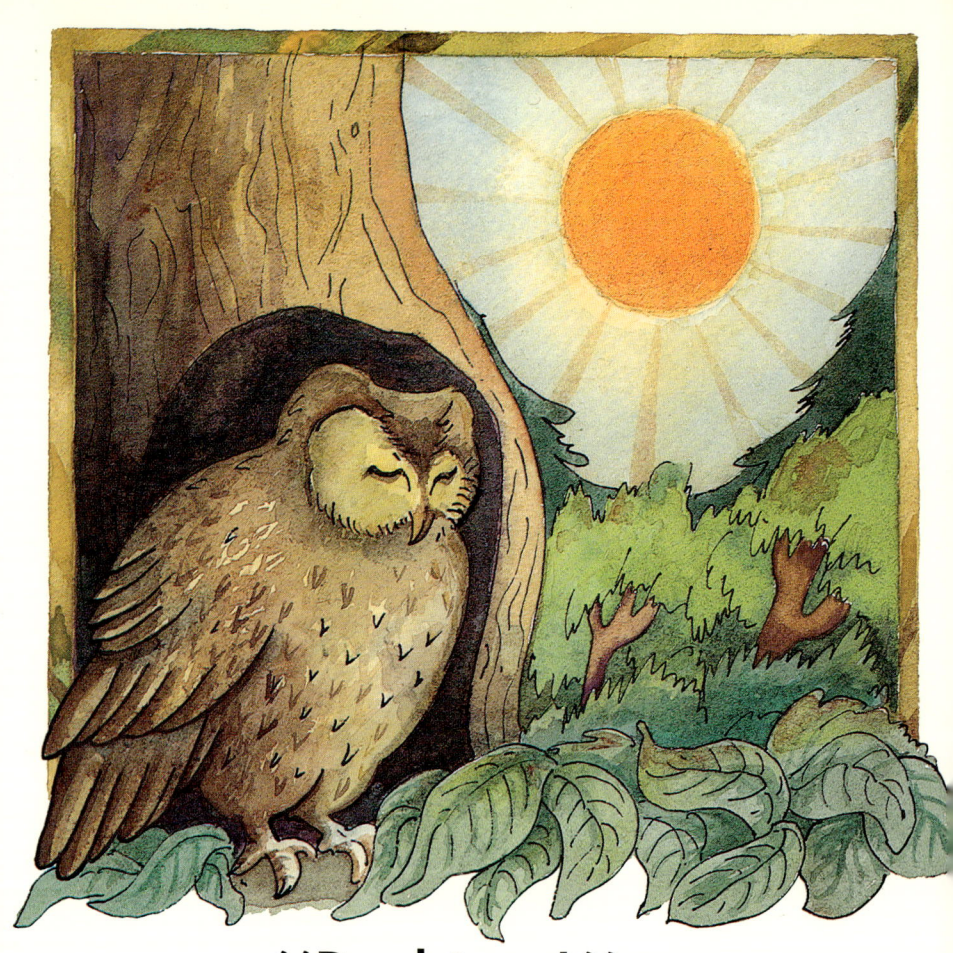

"Bedtime!"
said the owl.